SAVING
WILDLIFE

Woodland and Forest Animals

by Sonya Newland

A+

Smart Apple Media

Published by Smart Apple Media
P.O. Box 3263, Mankato, Minnesota 56002

Printed in the United States of America at Corporate Graphics,
in North Mankato, Minnesota.

Published by arrangement with the Watts
Publishing Group Ltd., London.

Library of Congress Cataloging-in-Publication Data
Newland, Sonya.
 Woodland and forest animals / by Sonya Newland.
    p. cm. -- (Saving wildlife)
 Includes bibliographical references and index.
 Summary: "Looks at endangered species of the world's temperate and boreal forest ecosystems.
Discusses the harm deforestation and hunting poses to these animals and suggests ways for
readers to contribute to conservation efforts. Includes maps, diagrams, and reading quiz"--Provided by publisher.
 ISBN 978-1-59920-662-2 (library binding)
 1. Forest animals--Juvenile literature. 2. Wildlife conservation--Juvenile literature. I. Title.
 QL112.N393 2012
 591.73--dc22
                    2010027175

Produced for Franklin Watts by
White-Thomson Publishing
Series consultant: Sally Morgan
Designer: Clare Nicholas
Picture researcher: Amy Sparks

Picture Credits
Dreamstime: Cover (Ekaterina Dushenina), 5 (Michael Woodruff), 6 (Kelly Boreson), 7 (Calamityjohn), 8 (Outdoorsman), 9t
(Oksanaphoto), 11t (Angel Sosa), 13b (James Hearn), 15 (Viktor Glupov), 18l (Eric Issele), 21 (Jason Kasomovic), 22l (Darren Green),
24t (Paulo Simão); **Nature Photo Library:** 9b (Pete Oxford), 11b (Yuri Shibnev), 13t (Shattil & Rozinski), 20b (Dave Watts), 22r (Pete
Oxford), 26b (John Downer); **iStock:** 23t (Clint Spencer); **NHPA:** 19t (A.N.T. Photo Library); **Photolibrary:** 12 (Christina Krutz), 14
(Helge Schulz), 17b (Bildagentur RM), 20t (Peter Weimann), 23b (Allen Blake Sheldon), 25b (Bill Beatty), 27t (Jared Hobbs), 27b
(Maurice Tibbles); **Shutterstock:** 10 (Tom Tietz), 16 (Wendy Nero), 17t (Susan Flashman), 18r (Bruce MacQueen), 19b (Jo Chambers),
24b (Charles Shapiro), 26t (RJ08).

Every attempt has been made to clear copyright. Should there be any inadvertent omission
please apply to the publisher for rectification.

1019
3-2011

9 8 7 6 5 4 3 2 1

Contents

Words in **bold** are in the glossary on page 31.

Woodland and Forest Habitats

Woodlands and forests are places where trees are the main type of plant. They can be found all over the world except in Antarctica and most of the Arctic, in deserts, grasslands, and on the very tops of mountains.

What Is a Forest?

In forests, the trees are very close together. Forests are often dark because the branches and leaves form a kind of "roof" that lets in very little sunlight. Woodlands are lighter because the trees are farther apart. Sometimes there are clearings in woods, where no trees grow and sunlight can reach the ground.

Black bear
(page 8)

North America

Salamander
(page 23)

Forest Types

There are three main types of forest—tropical, temperate, and boreal. Tropical forests, often called rain forests, are found in the warmest parts of the world, near the **equator**. Temperate forests grow in cooler regions. There are different types of temperate forests, including rain forests, but most have trees that lose their leaves in fall and winter. **Boreal forests** grow in very cold **climates** and are usually made up of evergreen trees. This book looks at animals that live in the world's temperate and boreal forests.

South America

Woodland Wildlife

Rain forests are home to more types of animals and plants than anywhere on earth, but thousands of species live in temperate and boreal forests and woodlands. Creatures as small as ants and as large as bears feast on flowers, fruit, insects, or smaller animals. In the cold winter months, some **hibernate** while others **migrate** to warmer parts of the world.

EXTREME ANIMALS

Woodpeckers—found in woodlands all over the world—can hammer up to 20 times a second when drilling into tree trunks.

▼ *Forests can be found in most parts of the world. Close to the equator are tropical forests. Temperate and boreal forests lie in cooler northern regions.*

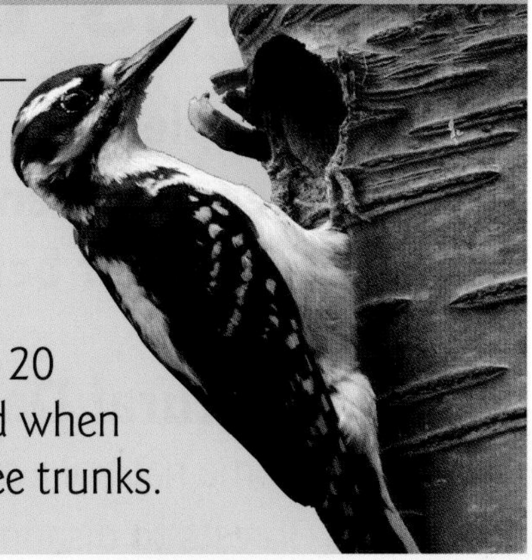

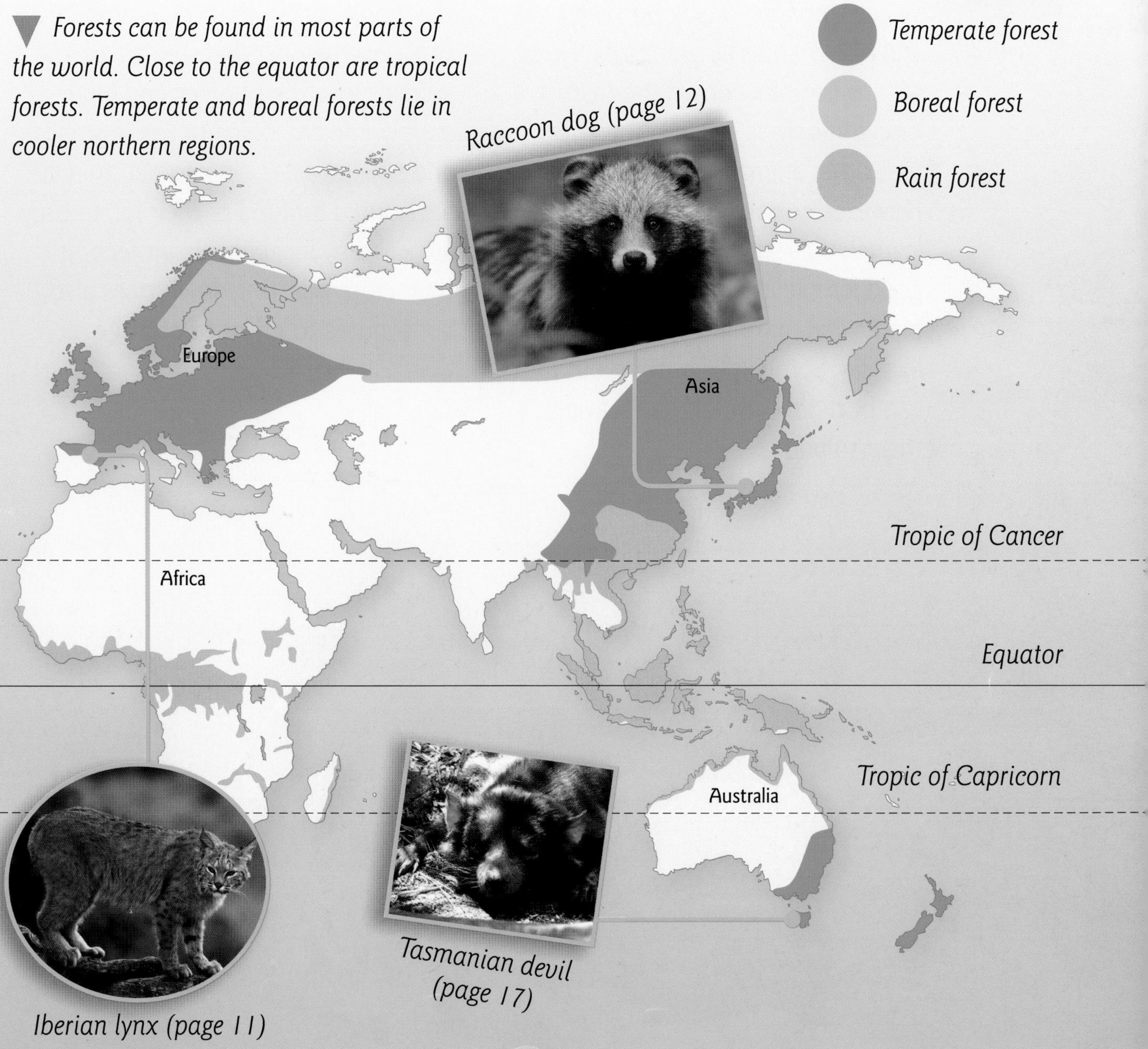

Temperate forest
Boreal forest
Rain forest
Raccoon dog (page 12)
Europe
Asia
Africa
Australia
Tropic of Cancer
Equator
Tropic of Capricorn
Tasmanian devil (page 17)
Iberian lynx (page 11)

Forests under Threat

People have always cut down trees, but recently this has been happening on a much larger scale and more rapidly than ever before.

Natural Dangers

Some natural events have caused forests to disappear. **Wildfires** can sweep through forests, burning trees and plants and killing animals. Fierce storms can blow down the trees. Insect invasions can kill off plants that other animals rely on for food. However, **conservationists** have learned that sometimes fires can be good for forests, clearing away dead plants and making way for new ones to grow. Sometimes putting out fires can be more harmful than leaving them to burn.

Human Threats

People are also threatening forest wildlife. They cut down trees to use the wood and so that they can farm or live in the once-forested areas. The animals lose their homes and food supply and are forced to live in smaller and smaller areas. Sometimes animals are hunted for food or their fur, or they are killed by local people protecting their crops. Cutting down trees also contributes to **climate change**.

▼ *Large areas of forest are cut down so that the timber can be sold.*

Web of Life

Everything in forest **habitats** relies on other living things to survive. Creatures such as earthworms help keep the soil healthy so plants can grow, providing food and shelter for wildlife. Insects such as butterflies and bees **pollinate** flowers. Small **mammals** and birds eat insects, and larger mammals eat smaller ones. This means that any changes can affect everything that lives there, so it is important to preserve this precious environment.

▶ *All woodland creatures rely on others as a source of food or to keep the soil, flowers, and trees healthy. This robin has caught a worm to feed her chicks.*

ENDANGERED ANIMALS

The International Union for the Conservation of Nature (IUCN) lists animals according to how **endangered** they are.

Extinct: Died out completely

Extinct in the wild: Only survive in captivity

Critically endangered: Extremely high risk of becoming **extinct** in the near future

Endangered: High risk of becoming extinct in the wild

Vulnerable: High risk of becoming endangered in the wild

Near threatened: Likely to become endangered in the near future

Least concern: Lowest risk of becoming endangered

Big Bears

Bears thrive in temperate forests. Their dark fur provides camouflage, and their thick coats protect them in winter. Bears will eat almost anything they can find in the forest, from acorns to animals as large as deer.

Black Bears

American black bears can be found in different habitats in North America—from mountains to open landscapes—but they prefer forests. They are good at climbing, so they can reach food that grows or lives high up in the trees. Black bears are not considered endangered, but because they are hunted for sport, their numbers are carefully monitored to make sure that not too many are being killed.

Brown Bears

Brown bears once roamed all over Europe and Asia, but not many survive on these **continents**, and in Europe brown bears are a **protected species**. The grizzly bear, a type of brown bear, is only found in North America. Many live in **national parks**, so they are safe from human threats, but others are suffering because of **deforestation** and hunting. The U.S. Fish and Wildlife Service is trying to increase the numbers of grizzly bears by breeding them in captivity and then releasing them to areas where there are not many left.

◄ *Black bears are protected by an international **trade agreement** that tries to stop illegal **poaching**.*

Grizzly bears can kill an animal or a human with a single swipe of their large paws.

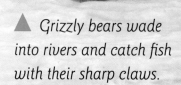
Grizzly bears wade into rivers and catch fish with their sharp claws.

SAVING WILDLIFE

Sloth Bear

Sloth bears of the **deciduous** forests of Asia are hunted or caught and forced to "dance" for entertainment. The World Society for the Protection of Animals (WSPA) is working with the Wildlife Trust of India (WTI) to stop these practices. They run public-education programs, rescue mistreated bears, and try to prevent illegal poaching.

Cats on the Prowl

Forests are the perfect habitat for big cats—they can climb well and move easily through the trees. Their patterned fur offers good camouflage so they can sneak up on their prey.

Forest Felines

Cats such as tigers and jaguars live in steamy rain forests, but many other types of cats—including bobcats, lynx, pumas, and some types of leopards—prefer cooler climates. Many cats are hunted for their fur or are killed because they attack **livestock** or simply because people are afraid of them.

▼ *North American bobcats adapt easily to different habitats, so they are not considered endangered.*

▲ With only around 100 left in the wild, the Iberian lynx is one of the world's most endangered cats.

Lynx on the Brink

One cat that has not survived hunting and habitat loss is the Iberian lynx, and there may only be around 100 of them left in Spain. The WWF (see page 28) is working with the Spanish government on a **captive-breeding** program. If this is successful, the lynx will later be released into the wild, saving the **species** from extinction.

SAVING WILDLIFE

Amur Leopard

There are 30–35 Amur leopards left in Russia and China. The Amur Leopard and Tiger Alliance (ALTA) is working to save these cats by stopping illegal poaching, educating local people, and protecting the leopard's habitat. **Conservation** programs have already saved the Amur tiger, so there is hope for this endangered leopard.

WHAT DO YOU THINK?

Farmers kill leopards because they attack livestock. To save the big cats, the ALTA pays farmers for any animals killed by leopards. Do you think it's right to pay people not to kill endangered species? Why or why not?

▶ Researchers in Russia attach a special collar to an Amur leopard so they can track it in the wild.

Wild Dogs

Trees provide good cover for wild dogs such as wolves, jackals, and foxes. Although they are not good climbers, there are plenty of animals on the ground for the dogs to hunt.

Protecting Raccoon Dogs

Although not yet considered endangered, the raccoon dog of Asia may soon be threatened because it is widely hunted for its fur, meat, and bones—especially in Japan. An island in Japan is now a protected area, set aside especially for these wild dogs. There are also now some raccoon dogs in northern Europe and parts of Russia.

▼ *Raccoon dogs are hunted in China and Japan so their fur can be made into clothing.*

Red Wolf

Habitat loss and illegal hunting have severely endangered the red wolf. There are thought to be around 300 red wolves left, and 200 of these only survive in captivity. They are being bred in the hope of increasing their numbers, and several programs are reintroducing red wolves into the wild in North Carolina.

▲ *This red wolf is in the Victoria Zoo in Victoria, Texas. Two-thirds of the remaining red wolves are in captivity.*

Dholes in Danger

Dholes are a rare species of Asian wild dog. They once ranged all across Asia, but deforestation has put them in danger. Animals that the dholes rely on for food, such as deer and wild pigs, move to other areas so the dogs are losing both their homes and their food supply. The Dhole Conservation Project is raising awareness about this little-known dog, and it is a protected species.

EXTREME ANIMALS

While many animals became extinct at the end of the last ice age around 10,000 years ago, wolves survived and have been roaming earth for more than a million years.

On the Hoof

Many types of deer and other hoofed animals once lived in the world's forests and woodlands. Although some have suffered from habitat loss and hunting, they are still found on almost every continent.

▼ *Male red deer are big animals, but they are still threatened by hunters, especially humans, who value their antlers.*

European Bison

By 1919, the European bison, or wisent, had been hunted to extinction in the wild. Luckily, some zoos had the bison, and captive-breeding programs helped it survive. Although they are still endangered, there are now around 1,800 European bison in the wild, roaming through the Bialowieza forest, which stretches between Poland and Belarus.

Natural Prey

Deer are hunted by many different forest animals, including big cats, bears, and wolves. They are sometimes even snatched by birds of prey. However, they are also popular targets for human hunters, who kill them for sport. As their woodland homes have been cut down, most deer have adapted to living in more open areas. Although this means they can survive habitat loss, it does make them easier prey for both animal and human **predators**.

Red-deer Management

Although most deer species are not under threat, many experts think that they might be in the near future because of deforestation. To stop this from happening, several countries have conservation programs. In the United Kingdom, the Forestry Commission works with local people to manage deer populations, and in Greece, WWF monitors the small population of red deer in the Parnitha National Park. This is especially important as the area suffered damage from wildfires in 2007.

Medium Mammals

As well as bears, cats, and wild dogs, several other hunters make their homes in forests and woodlands, including wild pigs, wolverines, and martens.

Wolverines look like small bears, but they are actually members of the weasel family.

Big Weasels

Wolverines live in northern boreal forests, where they feast on smaller mammals such as squirrels and rabbits. Suffering from habitat loss, hunting, and slow breeding, the number of wolverines has dropped dramatically in the past 100 years, especially in the United States. Environmental groups are campaigning to make wolverines an endangered species so they will be protected by law.

Running Wild

Wild boars thrive in woodlands because they will eat almost anything—from nuts and berries to small deer. In turn, they are preyed on by larger **carnivores**. They were hunted to extinction in many parts of Europe, but now some countries have reintroduced wild boars from other countries with great success.

WHAT DO YOU THINK?

The rapid increase in wild boars in Germany has caused problems, as the animals damage property and have even dug up graves. How could populations of animals like this be controlled? Should we be more careful when choosing which animals are reintroduced and why?

▲ *There are more than two million wild boars in Germany.*

Small Mammals

In the trees and in burrows on the ground, small mammals such as mice, rabbits, hedgehogs, skunks, and chipmunks feast on the plentiful plants and insects of their forest habitat.

Abundant Animals

Some woodland mammals are so abundant that they are considered pests, especially when they grow so bold that they move into urban areas. Others, including weasels and stoats, are deliberately killed to keep them under control. But all little woodland animals are affected by habitat loss and climate change, and when small mammals disappear, the larger animals that feed on them also suffer.

▼ *Woodland rabbits live in underground tunnels called warrens.*

EXTREME ANIMALS

American woodland skunks can spray their foul-smelling liquid with amazing accuracy as far as 11.5 ft. (3.5 m).

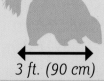

3 ft. (90 cm)

SAVING WILDLIFE

Smoky Mouse

The smoky mouse is found only in Australia, but the clearing of its forest home for timber and road building has made it an endangered species. The government of New South Wales in Australia has begun a recovery program, which includes protecting the areas where smoky mice still live, controlling the numbers of animals that prey on them, and educating local people about how they can help save the mice.

Save the Squirrel

Red squirrels are **native** to Europe, and there are still lots of them in many countries. In the United Kingdom, they are being wiped out by gray squirrels, introduced from America. There are now only 160,000 red squirrels—a small number compared to the 2.5 million grays. The Forestry Commission is researching ways to increase the numbers of red squirrels. The Save Our Squirrels campaign is also encouraging the public to help by reporting sightings of red squirrels to monitor populations.

▶ *In countries such as Finland and Russia, red squirrels are threatened by people hunting them for their fur.*

19

By the Water

Along the edges of woodland rivers and streams live a variety of water-loving animals. They often build their burrows in the riverbanks and feed on fish.

Otters on the Water

Otters live by the water but use nearby woodlands for breeding and **foraging** for food. In Europe and North America, water **pollution** and the destruction of woodlands have placed them under threat. They are now a protected species and are bred in special otter **sanctuaries** in many countries.

◄ *Water pollution is a big threat to otters and other riverbank creatures.*

SAVING WILDLIFE

Platypus

The curious-looking platypus of Australia's forests was saved from extinction in the early twentieth century by laws that banned their hunting. Although there are lots of platypuses now, experts are concerned that pollution and habitat loss might pose new threats.

Sandhill Cranes

Mississippi sandhill cranes make their nests in shallow wetlands of temperate forests in Mississippi. The Mississippi sandhill crane, along with 11 other species of crane, is endangered due to habitat loss. Many cranes lost their homes after pine plantations were built in the state, and now there are only 110 Mississippi sandhill cranes left. They all live in the Mississippi Sandhill Crane National Wildlife Refuge, where workers are trying to restore their habitat.

Beaver Builders

Beavers are very important to the woodland **ecosystem**. They are famous for gnawing down trees to build dams. This creates pools of water for them to live by and for other species to use as vital water sources. It also helps make room for fresh young trees to grow. Beavers were nearly extinct in some parts of Europe only 10 years ago, but people now recognize the important role they play in their habitat. They are protected by international trade laws and are not considered endangered any longer.

EXTREME ANIMALS

Once beavers start building a dam, they won't stop until they have finished. The largest beaver dam ever recorded was 4,921 ft. (1.5 km) long.

Slimy and Scaly Creatures

Reptiles and amphibians are at home in shady woodlands and forests. The damp ground, pools, and abundant insects for food are all vital for the survival of these creatures.

Cool Snakes

Although many snakes live in warm tropical regions, some of them prefer the cooler climate of northern forests. The black rat snake of North America preys on rabbits and rodents on the forest floor, but it can slither up trees where its dark skin helps it blend in among the branches. The timber rattlesnake, found in the United States' deciduous forests, is one of the most dangerous snakes in the country. One bite can kill a human.

◀ *Timber rattlesnakes are listed as near threatened by the IUCN, and they are the subject of conservation efforts by the Endangered and Nongame Species Program in the United States.*

SAVING WILDLIFE

Angonoka Tortoise
In 1993, there were only 100–400 Angonoka tortoises surviving in Madagascar's dry forests. However, thanks to captive-breeding programs and careful management of their forest habitat, there are now more than 1,000. They are still one of the world's most endangered animals, but it seems they have been saved from extinction.

Pond Life

Salamanders, frogs, and turtles are all at home in damp woodland environments. They usually live near pools and feed on insects on the forest floor. Among the most threatened **reptiles** are American box turtles. They are often caught as pets, but a bigger problem is **fragmentation** —when areas of forest are cut down, separating groups of animals.

▲ *As they try to get from one part of the forest to the other, many box turtles are run over by cars.*

WHAT DO YOU THINK?

One of the main threats to box turtles is climate change, and some people have said this is a good argument for keeping them in captivity where their environment can be controlled. What are the arguments for and against keeping box turtles as pets?

◄ *The endangered northern red salamander lives in deciduous forests in the eastern United States as far west as Ohio and Indiana.*

Minibeasts

Insects and other bugs play a vital role in the woodland ecosystem. There are so many species, however, that experts think there may be insects under threat that we don't even know about.

Insects Everywhere

On the forest floor, snails, worms, centipedes, ants, beetles, and many other minibeasts live among the decaying leaves, moss, and fallen trees. Worms help keep the soil healthy by creating tunnels that allow air and water to seep into it. Butterflies and bees carry pollen between flowers, which is important for seed production. Some insects even control other insect populations, such as caterpillars, which eat plant leaves.

▲ *Too many caterpillars in a forest can cause problems because they eat the leaves of plants.*

EXTREME ANIMALS

Monarch butterflies make one of the longest insect migrations in the world to and from their wintering grounds in Mexican forests. They travel up to 2,800 mi. (4,500 km) every year.

Spruce-fir Moss Spider

Tiny spruce-fir moss spiders live in fir forests in the United States, but they are being wiped out by an insect invasion from Europe. Balsam-wooly adelgids are killing off the fir trees, which exposes the moss in which the spiders live, causing them to dry out and die. Little is known about these spiders, but research is helping experts understand more, and captive-breeding programs have begun.

The Forest Food Chain

Insects are eaten by birds, small mammals, reptiles, and **amphibians**. If the numbers of insects drop, the survival of larger animals is threatened. In turn, even bigger animals come under threat because they feed on the insect-eaters. Conserving woodlands and forests will make sure these important creatures survive.

▼ *An American toad feasts on a large insect called a cicada.*

Birds and Bats

Woodlands are alive with the sound of songbirds in the branches. Owls nest in the tree trunks, and woodpeckers tap out insects. High above the treetops, birds of prey circle in search of food.

Songbirds

Songbirds all over the world are being affected by habitat loss and fragmentation. Some of them need quite large areas in which to nest and breed, so when their homes are broken up by roads and houses, they are unable to breed successfully and their numbers decline.

◀ *Songbirds such as blue jays are not currently endangered, but some may come under threat as more woodland areas are destroyed.*

SAVING WILDLIFE

American Bald Eagle
The recovery of the American bald eagle is one of the greatest success stories. The use of the **pesticide** DDT almost killed the eagles off because it got into water supplies and poisoned the fish that they ate. By the mid-twentieth century, there were only 417 pairs left. A huge clean-up operation helped reverse the damage. There are now more than 50,000 pairs.

Endangered bumblebee bats are some of the smallest mammals on earth—some are no bigger than a thumb.

1.25 in. (3 cm)

Keeping Bats Safe

Because they are sensitive to light and heat, bats are usually found **roosting** in cool, shady woodland areas. Many bat species are endangered and some are protected species in Europe and America, which means it is illegal to kill or injure a bat.

Night Fliers

Most owls are **nocturnal** creatures, nesting in trees or burrows in the ground. Groups try to protect woodlands to save endangered owls such as spotted and masked owls.

◀ *Owls such as this spotted owl use their coloring to blend into the background during the day.*

What Can We Do?

More and more forests and woodlands are being cut down every year, but people are more aware than ever before of how important it is to protect these precious environments. Sometimes national governments take steps to protect their endangered creatures. International organizations work with local communities to make a difference. But even individuals can help save woodland wildlife.

Find out More...

WWF (*www.worldwildlife.org*)
This is the United States' site of the largest international animal conservation organization. On this site, you can follow links to information on all kinds of endangered animals and find out what WWF is doing to save woodland and forest creatures.

EDGE of Existence (*www.edgeofexistence.org*)
The EDGE of Existence is a special global conservation program that focuses on saving what it calls "Evolutionary Distinct and Globally Endangered" (EDGE) species—unusual animals and plants that are under threat.

International Union for Conservation of Nature (*www.iucn.org*)
The IUCN produces the Red List, which lists all the world's known endangered species and classifies them by how threatened they are. You can see the whole list of endangered animals on the web site, as well as discover what the IUCN does to address environmental issues all over the world.

Convention on International Trade in Endangered Species (*www.cites.org*)
CITES is an international agreement between governments that seeks to ensure trade in wild animal species does not threaten their survival. It lists animals that are considered to be under threat from international trading and makes laws accordingly.

U.S. Fish and Wildlife Service (*www.fws.gov*)
This government organization was set up to manage and preserve wildlife in the United States. It helps manage wildlife reserves and makes sure laws that protect endangered animals are properly enforced.

World Society for the Protection of Animals (*www.wspa-usa.org*)
The WSPA is an animal-welfare organization with international campaigns to draw attention to and stamp out cruelty to animals, including exploiting creatures such as sloth bears for entertainment.

Do More...

Protect Local Woodlands

Find out what is being done to protect and conserve your local woodlands and the animals that live there, and offer your support. Simply going out and collecting litter can help keep this environment safe for wildlife.

Sign a Petition

Petitions are documents asking governments or organizations to take action on something people are concerned about. Some of the organizations on page 28 have online petitions that you can sign to show your support for their campaigns.

Celebrate Arbor Day

Arbor Day is celebrated on the last Friday in April to raise awareness of the importance of trees. To honor the day, plant trees with your family or class.

Go to the Zoo

Find out if your local zoo is involved in any captive-breeding programs and visit to find out more. Just visiting the zoo helps support these programs.

Adopt an Animal

For a small contribution to some conservation organizations, you get to "adopt" a woodland or forest animal. They will send you information about your adopted animal and keep you up to date on all the conservation efforts in the area.

Read More...

Disappearing Forests
Extreme Environmental Threats
by Corona Brezina
(Rosen Publishing, 2009)

Forests
Habitats
by Fran Howard
(Abdo Publishing, 2007)

Temperate Forest Habitats
Exploring Habitats
by Barbara Taylor
(Gareth Stevens Publishing, 2007)

Every effort has been made by the publisher to ensure that these web sites contain no inappropriate or offensive material. However, because of the nature of the Internet, it is impossible to guarantee that the content of these sites will not be altered. We strongly advise that Internet access is supervised by a responsible adult.

Woodland and Forest Animals Quiz

See how much you can remember about woodland and forest animals by taking the quiz below. Look back through the book to find the answers if you need to. The answers are on page 32.

1. What are the three main types of forest?

2. What natural events can destroy forest and woodland habitats?

3. Why are people cutting down forests?

4. Why are sloth bears under threat?

5. Which brown bear is being reintroduced by the U.S. Fish and Wildlife Service?

6. In which country do the only remaining Iberian lynx survive?

7. How is the ALTA trying to save the Amur leopard?

8. What animals do dholes eat?

9. Which country has a special island reserve for raccoon dogs?

10. How many red wolves are left in the wild?

11. What is another name for the European bison?

12. What natural disaster affected the Parnitha National Park in Greece in 2007?

13. What animal family do wolverines belong to?

14. Which disease is killing off large numbers of Tasmanian devils?

15. How many red squirrels are left in the United Kingdom?

16. Which species of sandhill crane is endangered due to habitat loss?

17. In which country can you find platypuses?

18. Where is the only place that Angonoka tortoises survive?

19. Which pesticide almost caused the extinction of the bald eagle?

20. Which bat is about the size of a thumb?

Glossary

amphibians cold-blooded animals that spend some of their time on land and some in water

boreal forests forests that grow in very cold climates and are usually made up of evergreen trees

camouflage the color or patterns on an animal that help it blend in with its surroundings

captive breeding when endangered animals are specially bred in zoos or wildlife reserves so that they can then be released back into the wild

carnivores animals that eat meat

climate the regular pattern of temperature and other weather conditions in a particular area

climate change a difference in the expected temperatures and other weather conditions across the world

conservation preserving or managing habitats when they are under threat or have been damaged or destroyed

conservationists people who work to protect the natural environment

continents the earth's seven great landmasses—Africa, Antarctica, Asia, Australia, Europe, North America, and South America

deciduous trees that shed their leaves in the fall

deforestation the cutting down of large areas of forest

ecosystem a community of animals and plants interacting with their environment

endangered at risk of becoming extinct

equator an imaginary line around the middle of the earth that separates the world into the Northern and Southern hemispheres

extinct when an entire species of animal has died out

foraging searching for food or other provisions such as material to build nests or burrows

fragmentation the breaking up of areas of forest by cutting down the trees between them

habitat the place where an animal lives

hibernate to sleep or move around very little in winter

livestock animals kept by people for meat or milk

mammals warm-blooded animals that bear live young

marsupial a mammal that nurtures its young in a pouch

migrate to move from one place to another; many animals spend the summer in the Northern Hemisphere but migrate south when the weather gets colder.

national parks special areas that are protected by national governments

native an animal that occurs naturally in a particular country or region

nocturnal coming out at night

pesticide a chemical often used by farmers to keep insects off their crops

poaching hunting an animal when it is against the law

pollinate to transfer pollen from one flower to another so that the flower can make seeds

pollution spoiling the environment with man-made waste

predator an animal that hunts others for food

protected species animals or plants that are protected by law so that it is illegal to do anything that threatens their survival

reptiles cold-blooded animals that lay eggs and usually have scales or plates on their skin

roosting when animals settle down to rest or sleep

sanctuaries special places where animals that are endangered or injured are taken to help with conservation or to be treated

species a type of animal or plant

trade agreement an agreement between countries about whether certain things should be bought and sold

wildfires naturally occurring fires that spread quickly

Index

Numbers in **bold** indicate pictures

Quiz answers

1. Tropical, temperate, and boreal; 2. Fires, storms, and insect invasions; 3. To use the wood and to make way for houses and roads; 4. They are caught and used as "dancing bears"; 5. Grizzly bear; 6. Spain; 7. Stopping illegal poaching, educating local people, and protecting their habitat; 8. Deer and wild pigs; 9. Japan; 10. Around 100; 11. Wisent; 12. Wildfire; 13. Weasel; 14. Devil facial tumor; 15. 160,000; 16. Mississippi sandhill crane; 17. Australia; 18. Madagascar; 19. DDT; 20. Bumblebee bat